D1520924

This book is a presentation of Weekly Reader
Books. Weekly Reader Books offers book
clubs for children from preschool through high
school. For further information write to:
WEEKLY READER BOOKS, 4343 Equity Drive,
Columbus, Ohio 43228

This edition is published by arrangement
with Checkerboard Press.

Weekly Reader is a federally registered trademark
of Field Publications.

WEEKLY READER BOOKS presents

What Is a Volcano?

A **Just Ask**™ Book

Hi, my name is Christopher!

by Chris Arvetis
and Carole Palmer

illustrated by
James Buckley

FIELD PUBLICATIONS
MIDDLETOWN, CT.

Why, that is
a VOLCANO!

Well, let me see.
First of all,
we live on the earth.
This globe shows what
the earth looks like.

Let's pretend
we can look inside.

Then we can see
what makes
a volcano.

It makes a path
through the cracks
in the earth.

1. MAGMA CHAMBER
2. VENT
3. GASES, ASH, LAVA
4. LAVA

The hot magma
that erupts
is called LAVA.
Rock parts like ash
and dust and gases
also come out
of the volcano.

And that's what makes a volcano. But, volcanos are not all alike.

Let's look at each kind.
In this kind, the lava
comes out of many places.
It builds a low,
broad mountain.

Oh, that's like
the one in Hawaii
called Mauna Loa.

Another kind looks like this.
This volcano has
a wide top and is made
by a big blast of magma
coming out of the earth.

That's like the
new volcano in Mexico
called Paricutin.

In each one, the magma
from deep inside the earth
works its way
out of the earth.
When the magma erupts,
a volcano is made.